# Introd

MW01709979

YOU THOUGHT MARRIAGE WAS GOING TO LAST A LIFETIME, BUT YOUR SPOUSE BAILED OUT. Your child chose a lifestyle you're not happy with. You had to put your career on hold to care for an ailing family member. A telephone call changed your life. A knock on the door derailed your entire day. Life doesn't always cooperate, and, if you're like many of us, you pout, complain, despair, and throw a good old-fashioned pity party.

Life disrupts. It isn't always what you want, but it's what you get. We all have to endure life's interruptions. Sometimes we go along for a while with just minor irritations, and then *WHAM!* A major, life-changing problem hits. We need to learn to accept the inevitable interruptions of life; there's no way around them. They are frequent, endless, and unavoidable, and we need to determine our reaction to them. It's all in how we choose to look at our circumstances that makes the difference in setting the mood for each day.

This Lent, before you react too quickly or sentence yourself to a life of despair and frustration, I invite you to give yourself room to breathe when interruptions turn your life upside down. When they show up, consider Jesus as your partner because he cares about these disconcerting interruptions. He offers hope as he reaches out to pick you up and get you back on your feet again.

I'm glad you're holding this booklet in your hands. I wrote it with you in mind. Take your time with it. Take the time to reflect each day, to do the activities, and to say the prayers. Let them refresh you. If your faith is a bit rusty, you are pages away from rekindling it by looking at your life interruptions with a whole new perspective.

TWENTY-THIRD PUBLICATIONS A Division of Bayard; One Montauk Avenue, Suite 200; PO Box 6015; New London, CT 06320; (860) 437-3012 or (800) 321-0411; www.23rdpublications.com

ISBN 978-1-58595-942-6 COVER IMAGE: ©ISTOCKPHOTO.COM/STAR55

JOEL 2:12–18 » 2 CORINTHIANS 5:20—6:2 » MATTHEW 6:1–6, 16–18

# Get busy living, or get busy dying

*When you fast, don't look gloomy.* MATTHEW 6:16

In the 1994 movie *Shawshank Redemption,* Andy Dufresne dreams of a life in Mexico. "Do you know what the Mexicans say about the Pacific?" he asks his friend Red. "They say it has no memory. That's where I want to live the rest of my life—a place that's warm with no memories." Red says, "I don't think I could make it on the outside, Andy. I've been in here most of my life." He ends with this phrase: "It comes down to a simple choice, get busy living or get busy dying."

As the fleeting years and circumstances pass by us, we sometimes forget how short and precious life is. Then something jars us, awakening us to the opportunity to reexamine our lives. Unfortunately, it is often a sobering event like death, financial loss, illness, unemployment, the end of a relationship, or a national tragedy.

Let's seize the opportunity before us—the season of Lent—to get busy living. There is no rewind button in life, but we can progress from where we are to where God wants us to be. Life is meant to be a celebration. Exercise wisdom by embracing every day as the treasure it is.

---

**WORK WITH YOUR HANDS** It is time to stop procrastinating. Call about that new job. Look for a larger apartment. Go to the park. Pamper yourself. Welcome that new relationship. Meditate regularly.

---

**WORDS FROM YOUR HEART** *Jesus, thank you for giving me this fresh, bright, gift-wrapped day. Amen.*

DEUTERONOMY 30:15–20 » LUKE 9:22–25

# Healthy choices matter

*Take up your cross and follow me.* LUKE 9:23

It happens: our health declines, someone dies, our spouse leaves, bills pile up, our children are prodigals. We can spend the rest of our lives sitting at home feeling sorry for ourselves. *Or* we can choose to rise above our self-pity.

God is impartial, providing each of us the same opportunity to have a good life. Some people are determined to grab on to that opportunity, and some are not. Determined people make healthy choices.

I once read that the only credit we get in life is for the choices we make. We choose to stay angry or let it go; to be envious or count our blessings. When things aren't going our way, we need to *choose* to get up, not give up.

If making healthy choices frightens you, remember that God is leading the way. Try adopting my personal creed: *God is in charge. God loves me. God never lets me down.*

Be still and *listen* to God urging you to use your inner strength to persevere and get back on your feet. Let this be your mantra: "I know this isn't going to be easy, but I'm never giving up, no matter how long it takes to cross the finish line."

---

**WORK WITH YOUR HANDS** During Lent, connect with a freshly bruised friend who is experiencing difficulties. Show up and offer a listening ear.

---

**WORDS FROM YOUR HEART** *Jesus, I won't give up as long as you supply the power to keep me standing. Amen.*

**MARCH 7 ~ FRIDAY AFTER ASH WEDNESDAY**

ISAIAH 58:1–9A » MATTHEW 9:14–15

# Sleepwalking through Life

*Can the wedding guests mourn as long as the bridegroom is with them?* **MATTHEW 9:15**

Lori was sleepwalking through life. Until her best friend was diagnosed with a life-threatening disease, she hadn't realized the grass she was standing on simply needed a little water. Can you relate? Are you awake, but always looking to the future to find fulfillment?

Your to-do list will never be complete—assignments to do, sales to make, things to save for, trips to take, people to see, work that needs doing. It's a never-ending treadmill. Problems arise when this pressure-filled existence prevents us from enjoying what is truly important—family, quiet time with the Lord, living faithfully in this world in preparation for the next, caring for and learning from others. When we live by the priority of the *urgent*, someday we will look back on a list of things we have checked off, but realize we have never really lived.

We spend so much time trying to be somewhere else—in another job, another relationship, another place. In our pursuit for greener grass, we miss life. The present moment is all we're certain of. Life is staring you in the face. Choose to live it right now.

---

**WORK WITH YOUR HANDS** No matter how far along you are in your journey of life, decide to take time for the important over the urgent. It's your life. Make it count.

---

**WORDS FROM YOUR HEART** *Jesus, help me take advantage of opportunities that arise, so I don't spend the rest of my life saying "I wish I had." Amen.*

# Keep pedaling

*Why do you eat with tax collectors and sinners?* LUKE 5:30

Are you sitting on the sidelines of life feeling washed up? Have you made mistakes and experienced setbacks and feel as if you don't have much of a future? I hear it all the time. *I have an addiction. I ruined my marriage. I failed in business.* A negative past doesn't make it impossible for you to have a bright future. No mistake is too much for God's compassionate mercy. If we continue to crucify ourselves, however, it will prevent us from receiving the good things God wants for us.

If we spend our time focusing on our mistakes, they can cripple us, causing us to cut our dreams short. *I didn't finish college. I didn't spend enough time with my family. I took my spouse for granted.* When we veer off course, God doesn't tell us "you blew it." Rather, God has a recovery plan for us—POA (Pedal On Attitude). He's cheering us on to keep on pedaling, so we can learn, adjust, grow, and improve. God is a God of another chance. You are not defined by your mistakes. Let them go. Be your best today...and pedal on!

---

**WORK WITH YOUR HANDS** Write on an index card an inspirational quote about moving past mistakes. On the other side, share a personal support prayer. Give it to someone who is living with regrets. POA—Pass it on!

---

**WORDS FROM YOUR HEART** *Jesus, you're always there to push, pull, or drag me through my mistake slump. Amen.*

GENESIS 2:7–9; 3:1–7 » ROMANS 5:12–19 » MATTHEW 4:1–11

# Let it go!

*Get away, Satan!*

**MATTHEW 4:10**

I frequently encounter resentful and bitter people. Something happened in the past and they have not forgotten. In fact, the pain of the event is surpassed only by the pain of remembrance.

Let's face it: all of us can come up with a short list of people who have hurt us. Someone spoke an unkind word or cheated us in a business deal. A parent was inattentive or abusive. Friends turned away when we needed them. A spouse broke his or her vows. Relationships are shattered because of people's cruelty. We all carry relationship-related scars, both big and small. So what are we going to do about it?

We could tough it out and pretend the offenses don't matter, but then something invades our thoughts and rattles our emotional cages. Some of us hold on to the anger and wish harm on the offender. But how you move forward is up to you: get over it or get even; heal or hate. Recalling the pain only makes it worse. Accept that it happened, take time to heal, and let it go. When the pain no longer owns you, you have the freedom to move forward.

---

**WORK WITH YOUR HANDS** Imagine yourself holding a trash bag open and placing your hurts inside. Tie up the bag and throw it away. Let it go. Forget about it.

---

**WORDS FROM YOUR HEART** *Jesus, with your help I will look at my pain, become acquainted with it, and then put it aside and move on. Amen.*

# Look at me, I'm here!

*Lord, when did we see you hungry or thirsty, or a stranger, or naked, or sick, or in prison, and didn't take care of you?*
MATTHEW 25:44

There is no shortage of hurting people in this world. There are those experiencing a serious illness, coping with the loss of a loved one, shocked by rejection or betrayal. They crave comfort and assistance from others. This is where our Christianity should fly into action.

We need to notice others, feel their hurt, and enter into their world. We need to look into their eyes and see their pain; we need to see past bad reputations and abrasive personalities and hear their silent cries.

Humans can't survive on their own. We need each other, especially in difficult times. A simple phone call can save a life. An occasional kind word or a ten-minute visit can be more effective than round-the-clock nursing care. Reach out and say, "I understand. I'm here for you. I ache with you."

The need to minister to the hurting is great. Look around. You'll see hurting people everywhere. While none of us can do everything, I encourage you during Lent to do something—visit, call, send a card, say a prayer, hug, do a kind deed. Sometimes, just being there for them is all someone needs.

---

**WORK WITH YOUR HANDS** Think of someone who might need a hug, and show that you care. Write the letter. Pick up the phone. Stop by their home. Your small act of kindness might make their day.

---

**WORDS FROM YOUR HEART** *Jesus, someone I'll meet today is lonely and afraid. Give me your words to bring them comfort, courage, and calm. Amen.*

# Favor yourself

*Forgive us our debts, as we also have forgiven our debtors.*
**MATTHEW 6:12**

Have you heard of the little boy who prayed, "Father forgive us our trespasses, as we give it to those who trespass against us"? When told to forgive, we think we're being asked to do something for someone who doesn't deserve it. It's not easy, because we think of the offense. Why should we let them off the hook?

Often, we want to lash back instead of forgiving. Lewis Smedes writes, "Forgiveness is spiritual surgery. You slice out your past damage that shouldn't be there." When we refuse, it comes back to us. I call this the "boomerang effect." When we throw out revenge, harsh words, or nastiness, they all return to us.

Do yourself a favor—*forgive.* When harsh words are exchanged and relationships harmed, settle the wrong and heal the hurt. Surrender your right to get even.

Remember, forgiveness isn't about them; it's about us. When we choose to rub it out, rather than rubbing it in, we can have peace in our lives.

---

**WORK WITH YOUR HANDS** Write down this prayer: "Compassionate God, I choose to forgive (*name the person*) for (*what they did*) even though I feel (*share the painful feelings*). Gentle God, I choose not to hold any grudges against (*name*) any longer. Thank you for freeing me from my hatred. Keep us both safe in your love. Amen."

---

**WORDS FROM YOUR HEART** *Jesus, I will rush to forgive anyone who has offended me, because I know the precious value of time. Amen.*

JONAH 3:1–10 » LUKE 11:29–32

# Enthusiastically you

*The people of Nineveh will stand up with this generation at the judgment and condemn it.* **LUKE 11:32**

When we leave our lives in the hands of other people, we never truly live. It's our responsibility to choose and define our own lives. Without others telling us, we already know what we need. We know what is important to us.

Often, others try to mold us into what they want us to be. After a while, we tend to give up, thinking they may know better. Occasionally, someone will resist and say, "No! I will not become who you want me to be. I want to become who I am."

I meet many people who are afraid to be who they are. They have layers of self-doubt accumulating, and they repeat to themselves: *I'm not good enough. I'm not smart enough. I'm not pretty enough.*

Why not replace those lies with a simple phrase and start each day saying, "I like me!" None of us want to stand before God as he asks: "Why didn't you become *you*?" That is our prime responsibility. God created us to be unique, with each of us having something to add to life that no one else can. Embrace *you*! Now that's something to get excited about!

---

**WORK WITH YOUR HANDS** Set aside a "Pamper Yourself Day" each month. Throw off your problems. Claim peace. You deserve these days. Give yourself permission to enjoy them.

---

**WORDS FROM YOUR HEART** *Jesus, I'm listening to your gentle voice whisper: "Become who you are." With you on my side, I will. Amen.*

# Prayer as ointment

*Ask and it will be given to you.* MATTHEW 7:7

For the most part, life is anything but easy. It's like eating an ice cream cone on a hot summer day—just when we think we have it licked, it drips all over us. Think about this: "Blessed are the flexible, for they shall not be bent out of shape." Prayer is the ointment that keeps our spirits flexible in the hands of God.

Use this ointment before bedtime to drain all the negative emotions out of your life. To live a wholesome life, it's necessary to drain suspicion, hatred, bitterness, resentment, envy, jealousy, and self-pity from our souls. Let's pray that Jesus will fill us with the healthy emotions of hope, humor, courage, joy, forgiveness, and self-confidence. Use this ointment to sustain yourself, to hold on and never quit in life.

How I love the words that were found, at the end of World War II, scratched on a basement wall alongside a Star of David. They had been etched by unknown German Jew in hiding: "I believe in the sun even when it's not shining. I believe in love even when I don't feel it. I believe in God even when he is distant."

This person knew the sustaining power of prayer. Even in dreadful darkness, this person basked in the warm sunlight of God's presence through prayer.

---

**WORK WITH YOUR HANDS** Tell God what you need. Keep praying. Every day. God is waiting to hear from us.

---

**WORDS FROM YOUR HEART** *Jesus, you are the hero of my soul. I love to talk with you in prayer. Amen.*

# One size does not fit all

*Make friends quickly.* MATTHEW 5:25

Our relationships have much to do with our happiness. We can have wealth and health, but if we don't have successful relationships, we're not going to really enjoy our lives. I've encountered people who are extremely successful, but they can't get along with others, so they're miserable.

Respect and consideration are essential in successful relationships. Sometimes, all it takes is making minor adjustments to see major improvements. Giving more compliments, truly listening, lowering your tone of voice, softening your words, and saying "I love you" or "I'm sorry" will significantly improve your relationships.

One size doesn't fit all. Healthy relationships come from an acceptance that we're all different, with different needs. When someone is upset, they need encouragement. Others need space; maybe we need to back off and give them a little breathing room. Some need constant affirmation. Learn what frustrates them or makes them happy. Most of all, learn to love them and not judge them. Experience them as they are, not as you want them to be. Grow with them and allow each new moment the chance to tell its own story.

---

**WORK WITH YOUR HANDS** Write genuine "pick 'em up" notes for your family and friends. Share quotes, poems, or Bible verses. Leave them on pillows, bulletin boards, backpacks, or car windows to encourage and build confidence.

---

**WORDS FROM YOUR HEART** *Jesus, help me take my eyes off myself so I can see what is going on with the people around me. Amen.*

DEUTERONOMY 26:16–19 » MATTHEW 5:43–48

# Difficult people! They're everywhere

*Love your enemies.* MATTHEW 5:44

Difficult people make us want to scream. We try to avoid people who get under our skin and irritate us. Sometimes, however, we cannot get away from them. It's as if they have been assigned to us by God.

They come in every variety—irresponsible family members, touchy co-workers, unreasonable bosses, cranky neighbors, snippy sales people, complaining customers, aggressive drivers, or self-important officials.

Some talk too much. Others have know-it-all and I'm-better-than-you attitudes. Some are the voices of doom and gloom, always critical and cynical. Some love to stir up trouble.

Usually, it's not us they have an issue with. They have an issue with themselves. Often they're hurting. They feel they've been slighted or wronged. Or they feel ignored and insignificant. Making things hard for other people is their way of trying to feel important, which they wouldn't need to do if they had a sense of their own worth.

Pick your battles wisely. Some things are worth getting upset about, and some just aren't. We cannot control or change difficult people, but we can refuse to let them rent space in our heads.

---

**WORK WITH YOUR HANDS** Make a list of difficult people. During Lent, pray for each person on that list.

---

**WORDS FROM YOUR HEART** *Jesus, give me extra helpings of love and patience for those who get under my skin. Amen.*

GENESIS 12:1–4A » 2 TIMOTHY 1:8B–10 » MATTHEW 17:1–9

# Fear fighters

*And Jesus came to them and touched them and said, "Get up and do not be afraid."* MATTHEW 17:7

"I'm afraid I'm going to lose my job." "I'm afraid my marriage is not going to last." "I'm afraid of the medical diagnosis."

I often hear these phrases from people whose thinking fuels fear and not faith. What we think about will take root in our lives. If we allow fear to take hold of our thoughts, we invite it into our lives and give it a right to become a reality.

Once inside our minds, fear dominates us, blowing things out of proportion. When we give fear a foothold, it incapacitates us, paralyzing us from our purpose. It trips us, making us tentative, uncertain, and hesitant.

Fear also traps us with lies. It is our responsibility to respond with confidence and say, "I don't agree." Most likely, what we fear will never happen. Obstacles that look permanent are only temporary. A setback is not final.

Stop fueling fear and start fueling faith, knowing that God can turn any situation around. With God on our side, we are unbeatable. Things may seem bleak and hopeless, but remain in faith, and God will heal and bring you through—better than you were before!

---

**WORK WITH YOUR HANDS** What beautiful opportunities is God seeking to bring to your attention? Be still for a moment. Listen. Then write them down and act on them—even if they seem impossible.

---

**WORDS FROM YOUR HEART** *Jesus, with you on my side, I will look fear in the eye and move ahead with my life. Amen.*

DANIEL 9:4B–10 » LUKE 6:36–38

# The right seasoning

*Do not judge, and you will not be judged.* **LUKE 6:37**

Your spouse was supposed to do something, pick up something, or get the oil changed in the car, but forgot. Now you're annoyed. It's time to watch what you say!

Our words should make people feel better about themselves, not worse. Our words should challenge others to press on to greater things. We should never use our words to make people want to give up.

If someone is struggling with something we have no difficulty with, what is the point of pointing out their weakness? Can being judgmental truly bring about positive change? Kindness, on the other hand, just might. When we're impatient for change in someone else, our attitude reflects our own character, not theirs. Our words have the power to build up or break down, to encourage or discourage, to heal or hurt.

Give others some slack. Just because we have strengths in certain areas where someone else has weaknesses, this does not give us the right to judge them and look down on them. We are to be the salt of the earth, but not salt in someone's wounds. Season your speech with love.

---

**WORK WITH YOUR HANDS** Read and memorize Ephesians 4:29 where Paul tells us: nothing unwholesome should come out of our mouths, but only what's helping to build up others. If what we're saying is not lifting someone's spirits, we shouldn't speak at all.

---

**WORDS FROM YOUR HEART** *Jesus, help me never to look down on anyone—except to help them up. Amen.*

# Preach what I practice

*For they preach but do not practice.* MATTHEW 23:3

"Practice what you preach," warns Jesus. But consider the words rearranged a bit: "Preach what you practice." Who we are and what we do each day speaks volumes! Our character shines through our actions. In order to preach what we practice, we need two things: *Good News* and *Good Works.*

We practice Good News by honoring God every time we bow our heads in prayer before a meal or praise God for the beauty around us. We practice Good News when we soothe a crying child, sit with an aging parent, reach out to a hurting person, or listen to each other. These habits of the heart show a Good News way of life.

We practice Good Works when we lend a helping hand to someone in need: drive someone to a doctor's appointment, teach a religious education class, walk in a marathon for cancer research, feed the homeless, mow the lawn for a homebound neighbor, take a meal to a widow, teach a child, donate to charity, hold a door, or simply say a prayer. These habits of the heart show a Good Works way of life that speaks of care, concern, and compassion.

Ask yourself: "Does my life preach what I practice?"

---

**WORK WITH YOUR HANDS** Let's remember that our lives *do* preach what we practice. So make a point to give good sermons this week.

---

**WORDS FROM YOUR HEART** *Jesus, help my life preach what I practice, using words only when necessary. Amen.*

2 Samuel 7:4–5a, 12–14a, 16 » Romans 4:13, 16–18, 22
Matthew 1:16, 18–21, 24a or Luke 2:41–51a

# We can't live without them

*Joseph her husband, being a righteous man*
*and not wanting to disgrace her....* **Matthew 1:19**

"When I was going through a tough time, I learned who my real friends were." I hear that a lot. Friends are the people who say, "I have your back," and mean it. They are the people who are there for us when the crowd disappears after a crisis. At a moment's notice, they drop everything and come to help.

Our loyal friends will stand with us through laughter, tears, good times, devastating illness, bad moods, and difficult circumstances.

They motivate us and speak the truth. Margaret told one of her friends, "Helen, you've been whining about the same thing for three months. It's time to do something about it." That's a true friend.

Faithful friends, special friends, and best friends are people with whom we have a connection of the heart. These people know us—shortcomings and all—and still love us. A true friend is a person with whom we don't have to pretend. We can be "real."

---

**WORK WITH YOUR HANDS** Choose a day before Easter and make it "Friend Appreciation Day." Prepare a package that includes a candle—to thank a friend for shining brightly when life was the darkest, a paper clip—in appreciation for helping you hold it together, and a chocolate kiss—for all the love your friend has shared with you.

---

**WORDS FROM YOUR HEART** *Jesus, when others walk away, my friends are there, healing my hurts and giving me hope. Help me do the same for them. Amen.*

# Ride the wave

*For I have five brothers—warn them, so that they will not also come to this place of torment.* **LUKE 16:28**

*I wish I had shown up on time. I wish I had spoken up. I wish I hadn't eaten that. I wish we saved money.* Regrets. We all have them throughout our lives. We look back and wish we would have done things differently.

Having a regret or two is normal. However, fixating on deep regrets long after we should have worked them out takes a toll on our health. The regret-ghosts will perpetually haunt us until we tell them we no longer have room for them in our lives.

Ride the wave of regret to engage change. If you are still stewing about how you treated someone close to you, ride the wave of regret and spring into positive action. Express sorrow. Make it a point to keep the behavior in check.

Lent is an ideal time to ride the wave of regret and make permanent changes. If you need to come clean with someone you hurt, do it. If an apology is needed, say it. If you need to make a choice, make it. Banish regrets and start with a fresh canvas. Be mindful of your actions and their consequences, and start to live your life...*regret free.*

---

**WORK WITH YOUR HANDS** Make a list of all your regrets. Then bury them in your backyard and forget about them.

---

**WORDS FROM YOUR HEART** *Jesus, I'm turning all my regrets over to you and asking you to wipe the slate clean so I can make the right choices today. Amen.*

# Hurting those we love

*Finally he sent his son to them, thinking, "They will respect my son."* **MATTHEW 21:37**

Do you remember the famous 1944 song "You Always Hurt the One You Love"? Some of the hardest blows in life are delivered by people we love. A spouse no longer loves us; a sibling turns against us; our prodigal child refuses to speak to us; a friend shares our secrets with others.

It's painful to be overlooked, disregarded, or ignored by someone we love. When we're deeply hurt, our first reaction may be to get even. We consider retaliating by starting a rumor or criticizing a character. Deep down, we know hurting another person will not resolve anything, but we're tempted to do it anyway.

Sometimes a hurtful word from someone is a cry for help. Listen closely. Ask them, "What's really going on here?" Provide a safe haven for them to express their feelings openly. Ask what you can do to restore closeness. Make an effort to explore and understand why they lash out in hurtful ways. Work to resolve the problem and restore the relationship.

---

**WORK WITH YOUR HANDS** Reflect on these questions: Should I allow someone back in my life who hurt me, or should I distance myself from them? Is there something I can say or do to make amends for a painful situation I've caused?

---

**WORDS FROM YOUR HEART** *Jesus, when you were hurt again and again by those you loved, you continued to love them and seek the best for them. Help me model your example. Amen.*

MICAH 7:14–15, 18–20 » LUKE 15:1–3, 11–32

# SING when angry

*Then he became angry and refused to go in.* LUKE 15:28

"He's refusing the court order to pay child support. All I want to do is get even." The mother was distraught. Unfortunately, she was allowing her husband's action to trigger the most dangerous emotion in life: anger.

We all lose our cool from time to time. Uncontrolled anger, however, can lead to problems at work, in relationships, and in the overall quality of our lives.

Next time you're angry, why not "SING" to safely release it?

*Stop* and notice your symptoms when you get angry. Look for signs.

*Imagine* the consequences if you lose control. By picturing the damage it can bring, we can diffuse anger before we snap.

*Notice* what sparks the anger. What are the triggers and buttons?

*Get away from the source.* Often our anger is so intense we cannot solve the problem until we cool down. Ask yourself: What can I do to calm down? Pray about it, and then take a walk or soothing shower.

Life is filled with frustrating moments. Harsh words are exchanged, feelings are hurt, and tempers flare. We can't always change the circumstances, but we can change our reactions.

**WORK WITH YOUR HANDS** Carry a small stone in your pocket. As irritation rises, move the pebble from one pocket to the other. This will help to interrupt the anger cycle and give you a chance to regroup.

**WORDS FROM YOUR HEART** *Jesus, enlighten me so I don't allow anger to control me as I prepare to confront a situation. Amen.*

Exodus 17:3–7 » Romans 5:1–2, 5–8 » John 4:5–42

# Be genuine instead of generic

*Many of the Samaritans from that town believed in him because of the woman's testimony.* John 4:39

"If there's anything I can do, just let me know." The words are automatic, and *generic*. Rather than resorting to the cliché, put your good intentions to work. Wounded people need kindness—a lot of it. And we are the ones who just might make a difference in their lives.

When Jesus walked into the life of the Samaritan woman, she was forever changed. Her life was a shipwreck. She either dumped or was dumped by five husbands and was working on her sixth. Yet she experienced caring kindness, not critical harshness, in her one-to-one encounter with Jesus.

Kindness changes people. Everywhere we go, a person can benefit from a smile, a compliment, or a kind word. People are no longer used to others holding a door, helping them with their packages, or simply doing another small act of kindness for them.

There is no age barrier for kindness. You can create a powerful impact that a person will remember for the rest of their life simply by doing an act of kindness. Maybe even you will remember it too.

---

**WORK WITH YOUR HANDS** Do little things that will help someone have a better day. Buy a meal for a person behind you at the drive-thru. Sit with a grieving friend. Smile and say "hi" to a passing stranger. Pay someone a compliment. Thank a veteran.

---

**WORDS FROM YOUR HEART** *Jesus, I want to keep kindness going. With your help, I can. I will. Amen.*

2 KINGS 5:1–15B » LUKE 4:24–30

# Bending over backwards hurts!

*No prophet is accepted in his own native place.* LUKE 4:24

Some people go to extremes to have others like them. They're nice, kind, reasonable, and devoted. They care, share, and give more than is fair. Their ultra-*niceness* stresses them out because of the motive—their need to fit in.

We can't make everybody like us. We can bend over backwards and some people still won't accept us. We can do everything they ask and it simply won't be enough.

The most difficult people to please are those with inflated egos and condescending attitudes. Jesus dealt with this attitude right in his own neighborhood. However, when they gave their hometown hero the cold shoulder, he didn't worry about what they thought of him. He said what he needed to say and moved on.

Jesus shows us we have the right to be ourselves. We don't have to please others or conform to their image of us. Stand up proudly and say, "Accept me for who I am or not at all. I'm finished jumping through hoops so you will like me."

Our value is in who we are. If we change just to be accepted, there will be no surprises, laughter, or creativity in our lives. Since everyone else is taken, it's best to just be yourself.

---

**WORK WITH YOUR HANDS** Write letters or cards of praise to someone who is feeling inferior and inadequate. Compliment them on their uniqueness.

---

**WORDS FROM YOUR HEART** *Jesus, help me see myself as you see me: a uniquely fashioned person of infinite worth. Amen.*

ISAIAH 7:10–44; 8:10 » HEBREWS 10:4–10 » LUKE 1:26–38

# The value of a promise

*May it be done to me according to your word.* **LUKE 1:38**

N*o way. It can't be. Joseph will be devastated.* Mary's thoughts must have run the gamut after Gabriel told her she was going to have a baby. She didn't get a sneak preview of how everything would turn out. Yet she chose to trust God and became a promise keeper.

A promise is a marvelous thing. When we make a promise, we reach into an unpredictable future and make one thing predictable: our promise. Keeping a promise is the most sacred connection we can have with one another.

Unfortunately, promises are broken. People don't show up, leaving us in the lurch when we counted on them. They persist in an old habit, even after promising to quit it. They even leave us after promising to stay for a lifetime.

Sometimes, however, promises are asked of us that we simply can't keep. When Annie's mother moved to a retirement community in Florida, Annie had to promise never to sell the family home. "With our own mortgage, car payments, and college tuition, it was too expensive for us to maintain," Annie explained. "I had to break my promise, and my mother was very upset with me."

Promises keep us close to those we love, but we have to know when the cost is more than we can pay.

---

**WORK WITH YOUR HANDS** Be realistic about what you can and cannot do.

---

**WORDS FROM YOUR HEART** *Jesus, I want to be a promise keeper. Help me keep my word whenever possible. Amen.*

# Kick it up a notch

*I tell you the truth.* MATTHEW 5:18

The woman was distraught. "My husband doesn't talk to me anymore," she said. "Night after night, he just sits there reading the newspaper or surfing through the television channels. When I ask him a question, he grunts 'uh-huh.' I could disappear and he wouldn't even notice. Why did we ever get married?"

People complain about their relationship; they take each other for granted or no longer engage in supportive conversation or joint spiritual practice. Their attention is elsewhere. They seem closed and unreachable. Whatever the cause, the relationship starts to grow stagnant after a number of years and the "honeymoon stage" starts to fade. Bored with their spouse, a person will save their best moments for work or for friends.

All relationships get to a point where the familiar and comfortable trumps the excitement that once was. If your relationship is heading down this path, jolt it with a spark of novelty to avoid ending up in a rut. Break away from familiar routines and sprinkle in some differences. Rather than going out for pizza every Friday night with the same friends, opt for Chinese with different friends. A bit of novelty goes a long way.

---

**WORK WITH YOUR HANDS** Make a commitment to bring something fresh into your relationship this Lent. Pretend it's your first date and see where that takes you.

---

**WORDS FROM YOUR HEART** *Jesus, it's time to get out of my rut and rekindle my relationship with the one I love the most. Amen.*

JEREMIAH 7:23–28 » LUKE 11:14–23

# Defusing the bomb

*Every kingdom divided against itself becomes a desert.*

LUKE 11:17

Imagine you are with the person you love and there is a disagreement. Immediately, the emotion kicks in that says, "I need to win this argument." It may be pride or stubbornness. It may be insecurity. "If I don't win, I won't be in the driver's seat." Maturity reveals there is a clear difference between winning the argument and winning in the relationship. Your goal should *always* be to win in the relationship.

Often, when a couple starts arguing, they see this as the beginning of the end. When you are in the heat of an argument, you can defuse it with two words—"I understand." Showing understanding is the key. You might not agree with the other person's reaction to a situation, but you can acknowledge where the feeling came from that led to that reaction. It is important to try to see where the other person is coming from before you go on the attack. When you attack first, without taking the time to understand, you can do serious damage to the relationship. Show you are on their side by being a team member and letting them know you understand.

---

**WORK WITH YOUR HANDS** Some researchers believe that couples who argue once a week have a better chance to stay together. Do you agree? Spend time together and discuss it.

---

**WORDS FROM YOUR HEART** *Jesus, as I grow in my relationships, I want to grow in understanding so I can see what the other person is experiencing. Amen.*

# A holy masterpiece

*The second commandment is this:*
*You shall love your neighbor as yourself.* **MARK 12:31**

It is a self-care platitude: "love yourself." Is it vanity? Arrogance? Misguided? No. It is actually a sign of respect and caring for this magnificent person God made you to be.

Truly loving ourselves is our awakening—a time in life when we finally get it by believing we are holy masterpieces of God who cannot be reproduced. No matter what our parents or teachers said, or what names we were called by schoolyard bullies, what really matters is what we choose to think about ourselves *now.* It's making peace with all the negative memories and feelings of hurt and pain. We can create our world and our life.

This Lent, begin to cultivate a healthy love for yourself by promising to stop self-criticism and watch the difference it will bring. When we start to love ourselves more each day, it's amazing how our lives improve. We feel confident and capable. Like chaff, our relationships are sifted—the negative ones carried off by the wind of positive change. Stand firm and declare that nothing can keep you from succeeding in loving yourself, God's magnificent creation.

**WORK WITH YOUR HANDS** Look in the mirror and say, "I love myself." How do you feel? Create "love yourself" reminder cards—"I love me as I am." "I'm a precious child of God, handle with care." Come up with your own sayings, and repeat them morning, noon, and night.

**WORDS FROM YOUR HEART** *Jesus, I need to love the person you intended me to be! Amen.*

HOSEA 6:1–6 » LUKE 18:9–14

# Disarming a know-it-all

*The tax collector stood at a distance and said, "God, have mercy on me, a sinner."* **LUKE 18:13**

Know-it-alls—we all know a few of them. They're arrogant individuals who think they're always right and everyone else is wrong. They're self-proclaimed experts on every topic or issue discussed. No one wants to be around them, and, when possible, we walk away, escaping with little more than some ruffled feathers. However, some situations are inescapable.

Know-it-alls—there seems to be one in every crowd. They correct us, try to one-up us, and perpetually interrupt us. While we should remain calm when around these know-it-all, finger-pointing, high horse "experts," it's hard to keep them from claiming center stage and getting us riled up. Let them know you're not going to take them seriously or hang on every word they speak. Dialogue is not parallel monologue; other people have a point of view and deserve the chance to express it.

End the conversation with "I have to go," or "thank you for sharing." When you cut the conversation short, you send the know-it-all a message, leaving less time to fall victim to their "wisdom."

---

**WORK WITH YOUR HANDS** Know-it-alls have little tolerance when contradicted. When you disarm them, it is important to tread slowly and cautiously. Before expressing your own views, soften your tone. Start by saying, "That may be true" or "Follow me with this." Their defensive screen is temporarily disengaged, giving you a chance to share.

---

**WORDS FROM YOUR HEART** *Jesus, knock me off my soapbox when I come across as a know-it-all. Amen.*

# The value of un-parenting

*Rabbi, who sinned, this man or his parents?* JOHN 9:2

The parents came to me for answers. "Our daughter's husband claimed bankruptcy, started drinking heavily, had multiple affairs, and eventually left," they said. "Our daughter is devastated. How do we help her through her divorce? What part should we play?"

Parenting adult children can be extremely painful, especially when life deals them severe blows. When an adult child's marriage ends in divorce, parents need to be supportive, but not patronizing. The same principle applies whenever children make poor choices. Perhaps you warned her not to marry a certain person. There is nothing productive about saying "I told you so..." when the marriage falls apart.

Back off and let your children live their own lives. However tempted you may be to step in and take over, avoid doing so at all costs. They need support now, not parenting.

Of course, you may need to help them financially. And, if divorce means single parenthood, help with child care. Keep in mind, though, you walk a fine line. You are needed—sometimes desperately—but wait to be asked. When your kids invite your advice or help, you can give it. Until then, just pray, and keep this in mind: advice is like snow—the softer it falls, the deeper it sinks.

---

**WORK WITH YOUR HANDS** If you have been emotionally devastated by the news of divorce, take time for yourself and get counseling if necessary.

---

**WORDS FROM YOUR HEART** *Jesus, you are the reservoir of strength when pain invades my family. Amen.*

# Surviving a hurt attack

*There was a royal official whose son was sick at Capernaum.*
JOHN 4:46

"M*other said there'd be days like this...she failed to mention they could go on for months at a time."* There's truth in this cartoon caption. Life hurts. It's not about the little bumps in the road. It's the big-time, life-rattling troubles that hurt so much we don't think we can face another day.

No matter what we're going through, the trouble is not here to stay. A failed relationship, layoff notice, bankruptcy, terrifying medical diagnosis, or the death of a loved one backs us up against the wall. It's OK to admit we're suffering and angry with God.

So, when we're raw, hurt, and bleeding, how do we find the gift of really living again?

Like the royal official in the gospel, turn it over to Jesus and say, "I need help!" This is where healing begins—when we quit depending on ourselves and welcome assistance. Let those with shared experiences offer their support and help you gain perspective about what to expect along the journey. That way the occasional dips back into the pits won't be as jarring. The pain will subside. You will make it through.

---

**WORK WITH YOUR HANDS** Make a hurt attack survival basket for a friend facing difficulties. Fill it with flowers, positive quotes, poems, Bible verses, or cartoons. Don't forget to include your phone number!

---

**WORDS FROM YOUR HEART** *Jesus, every now and then life will throw me a curve. With you to help catch me, it's easier to bounce back. Amen.*

# Right under your nose

*Get up. Pick up your mat and walk.* JOHN 5:8

"Complete mastectomy." The doctor's words shattered Julie's heart. "Chemotherapy and radiation to follow." Just then, a nurse friend slipped into the hospital room and, without a word, wrapped Julie in her arms. They wept together.

When we see someone we care about with problems, cares, and pressures of life, we need to drop what we are doing and go to them. Do not let excuses like "I don't know what to say or do" hold you back. It's not about fixing—it's about showing up, coming alongside them, interrupting their crisis for a moment, and hanging out with them.

There are no magical phrases that will alleviate their pain. Set aside the desire to give advice. Tune into their pain by listening. Giving your full attention is the best way to say "I'm here for you, right now. No one else, just you. I want to understand how you're feeling."

A hurting friend put it this way: "You listened as if you wanted to hear what I had to say. And that made me feel good."

---

**WORK WITH YOUR HANDS** If you suspect someone is going through a hard time, make the first move to call him or her. Suggest going to lunch, or invite them to your house. We need to learn to notice others who are openly hurting or are secretly lonely, sad, or struggling.

---

**WORDS FROM YOUR HEART** *Jesus, open my eyes to see the broken hearts around me. Amen.*

# Nothing lasts forever

*The Father raises the dead and gives them life.* JOHN 5:21

Death is stalking us. But, in many ways, facing the prospect of our own death is easier than dealing with the death of a loved one, particularly if the person we lose is young and seemed to have years of life ahead of them.

We stand at the cemetery trying to pay attention to encouraging words, and then we have to walk away, leaving the earthly shell of our loved one behind. Unfortunately, there is no way to avoid the experience of losing someone we love. Sooner or later, death pays a visit to every door.

Each time I visit a family that has just suffered a loss, I return to my car wishing I had known their lost loved one better. There are always dimensions of that life that surprise me. Sometimes, as we share, family members learn things they never knew.

There are unmined riches in every person we meet—blessings to reap, joys to share, depths to explore. We need to take the time to get to know each other...while we still can.

---

**WORK WITH YOUR HANDS** Get to know the people you love better. Start telling your stories to your family, or write them down. Make a point of asking others about their lives and dreams. People love to share their stories—all you have to do is ask.

---

**WORDS FROM YOUR HEART** *Jesus, I want to make the most of my life and the lives of others. Help me to cherish and celebrate life and love. Amen.*

EXODUS 32:7–14 » JOHN 5:31–47

# It feels like a bad dream

*I come in the name of my Father, but you don't accept me.* JOHN 5:43

Madly in love, Norma and Jeff enhanced each other's growth, built a home and family, and celebrated life. Then one day Jeff announced he didn't love Norma anymore, and he left.

Perhaps something similar happened to you. What can you do?

*Panic.* You can't believe this happened. You're shaken to your core.

*Predict.* Avoid the "ifs" and "maybes"—"If only I was more understanding, maybe she'd change her mind."

*Ponder.* Think of the experience as something affording you the opportunity to improve your relationship skills. List the things you enjoyed most about your relationship. Then list the things that disappointed you. Finally, list what you need from a relationship.

*Pamper.* Do things to calm your soul. Take naps in the sun. Read inspiring books that will strengthen you. Eat well. Take walks. Surround yourself with supportive people.

*Pardon.* Let go of resentment and hatred; they keep the wounds from healing. Don't generalize love based on your experience. Move on. Let the healing begin, one step at a time.

---

**WORK WITH YOUR HANDS** Make a list of everything you like about yourself: I'm an excellent cook; my garden is beautiful; I'm compassionate. Review the list. Pause at each entry and say, "Yep, I'm blessed with this uniqueness, and it will never leave me."

---

**WORDS FROM YOUR HEART** *Jesus, when my heart is broken, I'll give you the pieces to put it back together. Amen.*

WISDOM 2:1A, 12–22 » JOHN 7:1–2, 10, 25–30

# Laughing out the blues

*After his brothers had left for the festival, he went also, not publicly, but in secret.* JOHN 7:10

"He was a joyful peacemaker," the grieving mother said through her tears, describing her thirty-two-year-old son, who died in a tragic accident. Whenever people were arguing, her son would step in with a humorous remark. Soon the adversaries were laughing. The young man's sense of humor saved many people from becoming enemies.

When we start to loosen up a bit and poke fun at ourselves, the grim, painful, and frustrating moments of life seem bearable. Having a sense of humor doesn't mean we go around laughing at everything. We don't make jokes out of life; we only see the ones already there! We see the funny side along with the serious side.

Are you suffering from a laughter deficiency? Are you humor-impaired? Have you forgotten there is a lighter side to life? Laughter is the cheapest luxury we have. A good belly laugh expands the chest, lowers the blood pressure, clears the cobwebs from the brain, and gives our whole system a good cleansing. It is the sweetest music ever to greet the human ear. I believe God loves to hear our laughter.

---

**WORK WITH YOUR HANDS** Schedule a laughter-noon with friends. Share funny stories, watch comedy movies, and tell jokes. Create a slapstick kit filled with cartoons, amusing stories, all sorts of funny stuff. When you're wallowing in the blues, take it out so you can laugh them away.

---

**WORDS FROM YOUR HEART** *Jesus, I believe laughter makes life the merriest of go-rounds. Amen.*

# Look again

*Our law does not judge a man unless it first hears from him and knows what he is doing, does it?* **John 7:51**

An overweight, unkempt contestant lumbers awkwardly onto the *Britain's Got Talent* stage. The judges roll their eyes at the inevitable car-crash of a performance to follow—only to be wowed by the powerful, pitch-perfect voice of the unlikely star. Simon Cowell compared Jonathan Antoine's voice to the great Luciano Pavarotti.

We've all been guilty of the eye-roll, often missing the chance to go beyond appearance to see who someone really is.

When you meet someone, don't rush to judgment triggered by their skin color, clothing, accent, age, or gender. Look in their eyes and smile. See the person residing within—you just might see their soul. Allow them to be all they are and encourage them every inch of the way. This gives you the opportunity to share their feelings, desires, hopes, dreams, and pain.

Someone told me it is impossible to override the proverb about judging a book by its cover. While it may seem challenging, I'm not counting out the possibility that many people who choose to open the book and browse inside will like what they see.

---

**WORK WITH YOUR HANDS** Label a jar with the words: *Label Jars, Not People.* During Lent, drop a dollar in the jar each time you label someone. At the end of Lent, give the money to a favorite charity.

---

**WORDS FROM YOUR HEART** *Jesus, may I have 20/20 vision and see beyond appearances to the beauty of each person. Amen.*

EZEKIEL 37:12–14 » ROMANS 8:8–11 » JOHN 11:1–45

# Stepping-stones

*Martha then said to Jesus, "Lord, if you had been here, my brother would not have died."* JOHN 11:21

"My friends are always letting me down," Peggy shared, telling me how they repeatedly cancelled plans with her at the last minute. What should we do when friends treat us poorly? Perhaps we should follow Martha's lead: she confronted Jesus for not coming when Lazarus was dying.

You, too, can confront your friends, but be careful not to let anger seep into the conversation. If it does, you are bound to say something you will regret later. If you are too angry to speak rationally, wait a bit until you cool down.

Share with your friend how their behavior hurt you. Aim for understanding as you listen to their response. Empathy and compassion just might replace your feelings of betrayal and disappointment. Until you speak candidly with each other, you will have no way of knowing what might be happening in your friend's life. Understanding can be the stepping-stone toward forgiveness.

It might not be easy, but together, as friends, you can get through it. Genuine friends don't give up on each other that easily. They work it out.

---

**WORK WITH YOUR HANDS** Practice Jesus' teaching in Matthew 18:15. Gently confront a friend when you feel hurt, confused, or saddened by them.

---

**WORDS FROM YOUR HEART** *Jesus, keep my words soft and tender when I speak with my friend. Amen.*

# A healthy case of amnesia

*Jesus bent down and wrote with his finger on the ground.*

**JOHN 8:6**

Ever wonder what Jesus wrote on the ground as the men held stones? I think I know. Jesus was not writing, but scribbling and doodling; he was thinking, *These guys just don't get it. It's about second chances. Changing and correcting behavior. It's about conversion, not condemnation. The present, not the past. Forgiveness, not finger-pointing. It's about choosing to be a life-lifter, not a life-sinker.*

*Life-sinkers* aim to bring us down. They want to keep piling our mistakes, failures, and slipups on us, humiliating us with our past, throwing it in our face or rubbing our nose in it. They just cannot leave the past where it belongs.

*Life-lifters,* on the other hand, understand that we all mess up occasionally. It's unhealthy to keep replaying the painful moments over and over. Life-lifters walk with us and provide insightful opportunities to grow and improve. It's time to let go of the past and develop healthy amnesia—forget about it! Move on. Life-lifters believe what is in the past is the past, encouraging us and creating hope in our lives.

---

**WORK WITH YOUR HANDS** During this week, write thank-you notes to those life-lifters who have set you free from the crowd of life-sinkers. Write on!

---

**WORDS FROM YOUR HEART** *Jesus, help me remember you will lift me up and free me, just like you did with the frightened woman about to be stoned. Amen.*

NUMBERS 21:4–9 » JOHN 8:21–30

# Untying the "nots"

*When you have lifted up the Son of Man,*
*then you will realize that I am he.* JOHN 8:28

Two of the most powerful words are *I AM*. Why? Because what follows those two words defines who we are and what we are capable of doing. Many of us are conditioned to say, "I am not…," setting us up for failure before we even try. "I am not smart enough to succeed." "I am not worth a healthy relationship."

Overcoming the *I am not* mentality starts with trusting yourself and believing there are no limits to what you can achieve. Eliminate the *nots* from your vocabulary and start your sentences with "I am…" "I am capable of landing this job." "I am loveable." Whatever you choose to attach to the *I AM* will find its way into your life. This small phrase has the power to limit you…or set you free!

*I AM* is our real nature. It's genuine. It is truly who we are. No one else can say "I am…" for us. Only we can determine our own fate and destiny by what we attach to the *I AM*. It reveals what we really believe about ourselves. Every time you say you will not be bullied by fears, put-downs, or criticisms, you are improving your life. Your *I AM* is the catalyst of change that produces a healthy, peaceful, and happy life.

**WORK WITH YOUR HANDS** Brainstorm what you would attach to your *I AM*.

**WORDS FROM YOUR HEART** *Jesus, help me think of myself as you think of me—loveable and special. Amen.*

# Breaking the Pinocchio cycle

*You will know the truth, and the truth will set you free.* JOHN 8:32

Theresa's relationship with her husband was at the breaking point. "He's always covering up his mistakes with lies," she said. "Even when it's easy for him to tell the truth, he chooses to lie."

It's tough to be in a relationship with someone who lies. It's not about how we *feel* about them; it's just that we cannot connect as trust evaporates.

People lie for a variety of reasons—mostly to cover up their wrongdoings or to gain an advantage. From little white lies to major lies, the result of lying is someone getting hurt. Have you ever been in a relationship where someone was deceitful, often twisting words and exaggerating emotions? You knew, somewhere inside you, that something wasn't right. Once you get caught in the net of lies, all conversations have to support those lies, and eventually you tend to start believing them.

To break free from the net, you have to be up-front, transparent, and a teller of truth. Speaking the truth will improve your relationships. When you candidly level with others, you grow closer to them, and you never have to struggle to remember what you said.

---

**WORK WITH YOUR HANDS** If a relationship has been harmed because of a lie, plan how to restore it. Create a strategy and stick to it. Post this where you'll see it often: **TACT**—*Tell the absolute, complete truth.*

---

**WORDS FROM YOUR HEART** *Jesus, only telling the truth will free me to grow my relationships in trust. Amen.*

GENESIS 17:3–9 » JOHN 8:51–59

# Eleven simple words

*Amen, I say to you, whoever keeps my word will never see death.* JOHN 8:51

In his book *The Four Things That Matter Most,* Ira Byock puts his finger on some simple truths we all should practice. Eleven of the most important words ever spoken to heal relationships and bring closure are: Please forgive me. I forgive you. Thank you. I love you.

These four simple sentences express reconciliation, gratitude, and affection. They are words people *need* to hear and weave into their daily lives.

Bitter sibling rivalry, shocking family secrets, important matters swept under the rug and left unresolved—relationships can be rough and raw from unfinished business. A child doesn't speak with his or her parents for years. A mother carries guilt about punishing her daughter. A wife harbors unforgiveness toward her husband. A son believes his parents loved his brother more.

Relationships left with hostility, division, and brokenness will haunt your life unless you sit down and talk about it. Sharing buried feelings and expressing the eleven words above will soothe and mend even the most profound separations from people you love.

---

**WORK WITH YOUR HANDS** Don't wait until someone is on the brink of dying; talk it out now. Things left unsaid will bring a tidal wave of grief.

---

**WORDS FROM YOUR HEART** *Jesus, give me the strength to say what I need to say for peace in my life and relationships. Amen.*

# Drawing the line

*They tried again to arrest him, but he escaped their power.*
**John 10:39**

A couple I counseled engaged in relentless verbal battles, seriously contaminating their relationship. When the three of us sat down, we delved into ways to bring about healthy change, starting with a list of behaviors that enabled growth and reinforced clearly defined boundaries.

In order to protect ourselves, we must carve stronger boundaries and stop boundary crossers in their tracks the second they overstep. Put an end to their repulsive behavior by refusing to let them try to make you feel angry, inferior, violated, or frustrated. Put your foot down and firmly state, "I'm not going to put up with the way you talk to me or treat me anymore." Stress consequences—"If you do that again, I will..."

Jesus was a boundary carver. Once the boundaries were established, he didn't back down. He backed up his words with action. Setting boundaries is a way to fully honor and respect yourself. It will make a powerful impact on the quality of your life and relationships.

---

**WORK WITH YOUR HANDS** Complete the following statements: People may no longer _____________. I have a right to ask for _______________. To protect myself, it's okay to _______________. List at least six examples of boundaries you plan to set to honor yourself. Select the easiest, communicate it, and strengthen your boundaries.

---

**WORDS FROM YOUR HEART** *Jesus, I want to forgive those who have crossed the line and hurt me. I need strength to maintain my boundaries so it won't happen again. Amen.*

# Count your blessings

*What are you going to do? This man is performing many signs and people are believing in him.* JOHN 11:47–48

Diane wistfully talked about her friend's new house. "We have a wonderful house," her husband reminded her. "Many people would give anything to have what we have. What else could you possibly want?"

"More," she grumbled.

Envy is often concealed. Hidden under a smile, feelings of emptiness erupt from deep inside. Often confused with jealousy, which is the fear of losing our love to another, envy is in a class all by itself. It is a strong craving and desire for the possessions and qualities of another's wisdom, kindness, success, or looks.

We can choose to spend our time envying some rich and powerful person, the wealthy husband's wife who doesn't have to work, or the relative who just inherited a large estate from her mother—or we can get up every single day and count our blessings by focusing on the gifts we have.

We can curb envy by cherishing the people in our lives and the talents we have been given. If you are trying to rein in envy, remember the wisdom of Claudian, the fourth-century Latin poet: "Those who envy are always poor."

---

**WORK WITH YOUR HANDS** Start a gratitude journal. Every day for one week, write down the blessings for which you are grateful. Before going to sleep, offer thanks to God for them.

---

**WORDS FROM YOUR HEART** *Jesus, a funny thing happens when I count my blessings. The more I count, the more they show up. Amen.*

# Bitten by the betrayal bug

*What are you willing to give me to betray him to you?*

**MATTHEW 26:15**

Betrayal happens to all of us eventually. Sometimes it catches us by surprise; other times we sense it coming. Intimacy breaks down, compromising trust and security. It stings—especially when we have invested in a relationship only to end up being hurt.

Many people move through the same emotional process:

*Surprise*: "I can't believe this happened!"

*Seclusion*: "Who needs people anyway? They just let you down."

*Sorry*: "I should have listened to so-and-so."

*Sore*: "I'm so angry, I could..."

*Seething*: "I'll get even someday. They'll pay for what they did."

*Soothe*: "I want to be free from the pain."

This week, we encounter Judas' notorious betrayal and Peter's equally notorious denial of Jesus. Yet Jesus forgave.

For safety and sanity in our lives, forgiveness is the cure. This doesn't mean we condone what happened or necessarily let the betrayer back into our lives. It means releasing all the hurtful feelings trapped inside. If we choose to continue the relationship, it takes talking, time, and tenderness to regain the lost trust.

---

**WORK WITH YOUR HANDS** Take some time off and surround yourself with people who love you. Allow them to help restore you.

---

**WORDS FROM YOUR HEART** *Jesus, you're no stranger to having people let you down. I want to grow in trust again. Amen.*

# Forget about yourself

*Mary then took a pound of very costly perfume of pure nard and anointed the feet of Jesus and wiped his feet with her hair.*
JOHN 12:3

Obsessing over their own perceived "worth," some people spend a good deal of time thinking about how their job doesn't pay them enough. They are constantly looking out for number one, trying to get what they think they deserve.

We live with a "what's in it for me?" attitude. Judas had this same insatiable mind-set, and he drowned in his own selfish waters of betrayal, washing up on the shores of remorse and regret.

We need to be relentless against selfishness, refusing to live self-centered lives. When we care about only ourselves, we live in absolute misery. On the other hand, when we take our mind off ourselves and actively reach out to other people, we begin to experience true joy and peace.

Who do you know who needs encouragement? Is someone feeling abandoned or alone? Did they lose their job? Are they on the brink of bankruptcy? Smile at them. Give them a hug. Offer to babysit for them. Pay their utility bill *anonymously*. Find someone you can help, and forsake living a self-centered existence. There is no greater feeling than going to bed at night knowing you did something to improve another's life.

---

**WORK WITH YOUR HANDS** Think of someone in need. Show them you care. Write to them, call them, visit them. Your act of kindness will change their day.

---

**WORDS FROM YOUR HEART** *Jesus, I know I'm going to meet someone today in need. Don't let me miss the opportunity to help. Amen.*

ISAIAH 49:1–6 » JOHN 13:21–33, 36–38

# Drain the pain

*Jesus was deeply troubled.* JOHN 13:21

"God, will I ever stop hurting?" Barry asked months after returning home to discover that his wife left with the children.

When hopes are shattered, don't throw in the towel. *Drain the pain.* These three suggestions may help:

*Cry it out.* Let the tears flow. As you feel the pain drain from your body, healing will begin.

*Talk it out.* Initially, hurting people often say, "I can't talk about it." Eventually, however, you need to have a heart-to-heart with someone you can trust. Find a good listener who can accept your feelings without trying to explain them away or "fix" the problem.

*Write it out.* It's okay to be angry at God, but get those deep hurts out. Resentment, hatred, bitterness, and vengeance are emotions that cause radioactive fallout that will undermine your health. Release those negative feelings and write them out in a journal.

When the bottom falls out and nothing seems secure, stop pretending everything is fine; admit it hurts. Jesus did! Jesus will walk alongside you and give you the reassurance you need to continue. After all, he's not a stranger to feeling "troubled."

---

**WORK WITH YOUR HANDS** When life troubles you and turns your world upside down, cry, talk, write, and remember: *This, too, will pass.*

---

**WORDS FROM YOUR HEART** *Jesus, nothing will happen today that you and I together can't handle. Amen.*

# A bygone ideal?

*The teacher says: "My appointed time is near. I am going to celebrate the Passover with my disciples."*

**MATTHEW 26:18**

"Since my son is a single dad with two teenagers, we've been having Sunday dinner together for years," a wise woman told me. "During that time, I've seen changes in my grandsons. They say, 'please' and 'thank you,' and clear the table without being asked. Sometimes they even help me fix dinner."

We've all heard the saying *Families that pray together stay together.* It's also true that families who *dine* together are emotionally and spiritually *fine* together. Basketball practices, dance rehearsals, meetings, etc. make family mealtimes seem outdated. However, many parents believe it is the glue that holds them together. The family table is the place we come to engage each other, share wisdom, solve problems, confess, conspire, laugh, forgive, and repair.

So turn off the television. Put away the cell phone. Slow down, gather the family together tonight, and bow your heads to thank God for the meal before you—and for the people beside you.

---

**WORK WITH YOUR HANDS** Create family placemats. Have the children draw a picture to color. Add puzzles or trivia facts. The adults may want to add birthday wishes, inspirational quotes, or prayers. During dinner, allow each person to share his or her unique creation.

---

**WORDS FROM YOUR HEART** *Jesus, dinnertime allows us to shut out the rest of the world and pay attention to those who matter the most to us—our family. Amen.*

EXODUS 12:1–8, 11–14 » 1 CORINTHIANS 11:23–26 » JOHN 13:1–15

# What will they say when you are gone?

*For I give you an example, that you also should do as I did to you.* **JOHN 13:15**

I watched two elderly gentlemen exchanging greetings at McDonalds. "I enjoy watching my grandson," one told the other. "I hope he remembers me."

It's a huge question: *How do you want to be remembered?* At the end of your life, when everything falls away, what remains for people to remember? What words will people use when remembering you? If the litany of adjectives includes "kind," then I believe you have lived a life worthy of remembrance. Kindness is the core to a good, meaningful life—goodwill in a school, parish, and community. It isn't complicated; it's natural and only requires we pay attention to those around us who are crying out for help. Kindness motivates others to overcome their obstacles and pursue their passions with enthusiasm. What lives beyond us after we pass on will be the lives we touched and changed through thoughtful and compassionate gentleness.

---

**WORK WITH YOUR HANDS** As you go about your day, ask yourself, "How do I want to be remembered?" Then live accordingly.

---

**WORDS FROM YOUR HEART** *Jesus, I want to be remembered for three things: kindness, kindness, and kindness. Amen.*

ISAIAH 52:13—53:12 » HEBREWS 4:14–16; 5:7–9 » JOHN 18:1—19:42

# Whatever, Lord!

*You have no power over me.* JOHN 19:11

Whether I am praying with parents at a cemetery as they say goodbye to their child, supporting a parishioner as the doctor says there is nothing else they can do, or listening to a spouse mourn the loss of a marriage, I find it humbling to consider the magnitude of trouble in people's lives. But I'm encouraged as I watch them emerge changed, but better.

It's easy to hit the panic button and remain helpless, trapped in our troubles. Unfortunately, I can't offer a magic formula for making troubles vanish. After all the feeling, thinking, and talking, two words help: *Whatever, Lord!* He will get you through it somehow, no matter how ridiculous it may seem. Hand it over to Jesus; he's still in control.

Success in life doesn't reveal our true character; life's trouble does. While troubles are inevitable, misery is optional. When the storms of life threaten to bury you, remember: Jesus calms storms. Anchor yourself to him. Once the storm subsides and you realize you made it, help someone else who is suffering and stressed-out.

---

**WORK WITH YOUR HANDS** Pray and push. Spend time today in prayer. Reflect on the trouble spots in your life and turn them over to Jesus. Take a nail and squeeze all your troubles into it. Go outside, push the nail into the ground, and forget where you buried it.

---

**WORDS FROM YOUR HEART** *Jesus, it's a comfort to know you have your hands on the steering wheel of my troubles. Amen.*

GENESIS 1:1—2:2 OR 1:1, 26-31A GENESIS 22:1-18 OR 22:1-2, 9A, 10-13, 15-18 EXODUS 14:15—15:1 ISAIAH 54:5-14 ISAIAH 55:1-11 BARUCH 3:9-15, 32—4:4 EZEKIEL 36:16-17A, 18-28 ROMANS 6:3-11 MATTHEW 28:1-10

# We don't have forever

*He is not here; for he has been raised, as he said.* MATTHEW 28:6

Life is what we make of it, regardless of what we're given. Unlike a movie, life's script has no preview. We have to be active in the writing without ever knowing the exact ending. This is the exciting part of living: the rewriting of our scenario. Unexpected encounters occur, and the full plot is yet to unfold.

It's never too late to create the life you want. You can do it. It's not about a goal; it's about a process. You get there step-by-step. Embrace, enjoy, adapt, and adjust to what's along the way. Don't reach the point of death and realize you never actually *lived.* Squeeze every ounce of living out of life while you can!

Along the way, don't look over people's shoulders; look into their eyes. Enjoy simple pleasures and beauty. Hold and hug others. Do it now; these moments don't last forever. They're disappearing quickly and will never come again. There are many more waiting for you. Seize them. Now! Happy Easter!

**WORK WITH YOUR HANDS** Encourage those around you who are simply existing and not enjoying life. Give them a packet of flower seeds to remind them of the endless possibilities of new growth and fresh starts. Let them know it's never too late to start living.

**WORDS FROM YOUR HEART** *Jesus, I've never seen this day before; I want to live every moment of it without regret. Amen.*

ALSO BY

# Father Joe Sica

## Forgiveness

*One Step at a Time*

After twenty-five years of priestly ministry, and after counseling hundreds of people, Father Joe has concluded that over ninety percent of troubled relationships result from the unwillingness or inability to forgive. Here he offers ten invaluable steps to help you take forgiveness seriously, and he has choreographed them beautifully to connect with Jesus' teaching about forgiveness.

**152 pages, $12.95 (order 957620)**

## Embracing Change

*10 Ways to Grow Spiritually and Emotionally*

Here's a bestselling resource for all those who want to make positive changes in their lives. This is not just another self-help fix, but rather a self-care solution, a guide to revealing the person we really want to be. It's inspiring, challenging, and motivating!

**136 pages, $12.95 (order 952486)**

**ORDER ONLINE AT**

**www.23rdpublications.com**

**OR CALL 800-321-0411**